Sight-Sing a Song! 2

By Audrey Snyder

MORE MUSIC READING FOR THE ELEMENTARY CLASSROOM

T0061377

SET 2: KEYS OF D AND G

Table of Contents

HAL•LEONARD® CORPORATION

7777 W. BLUEMOUND RD. P.O. BOX 13819 MILWAUKEE, WI 53213

Visit Hal Leonard Online at
www.halleonard.com

Introduction

You've heard this question time and again...
this cry for help... this S.O.S. signal...

How can I teach my students to sight-sing when I have them for such a limited class time?

Perhaps you are the one asking it. Your request has been heard.

Sight-Sing a Song will help you do just that—teach your students to sight-sing with confidence. This well-designed sight-singing approach progresses in an easy step-by-step fashion through a variety of exercises that culminates with a special song students will be able to sight-sing on sight! Each lesson includes helpful Teacher Tips that focus on the music concepts being presented, a suggested teaching sequence to use when presenting each exercise, keys to sight-singing success, options for enrichment and motivation, and two student reproducible pages filled with sight-reading exercises. Exercises and songs are presented in the keys of D major and G major. After students have perfected each exercise *a cappella* on their own, they can enhance the learning process further by performing with the rhythm accompaniment tracks on the enclosed CD. Performance/ accompaniment tracks for the songs are also included.

For teachers who have used Set 1, use the first lesson as a rhythm review. The rest of the lessons will be new material. For teachers who are new to this series, this material for students starts at the beginning and assumes no previous sight-singing knowledge. You can start right now!

Good luck to you! Your S.O.S. signal has been answered!

About the Writer
Audrey Snyder

Audrey Snyder, an exclusive Hal Leonard Corporation choral composer, arranger and editor, completed her Bachelor's and Master's degrees in Music Education from the University of Oregon and did additional post-graduate work in England. During her many successful years as a public school music teacher, she began to write choral music for her own students, publishing her first choral piece in 1978. Since that time Audrey has published numerous original choral compositions and arrangements spanning the entire spectrum of choral music from Top 40 pop to the classics and from elementary through college levels.

Audrey writes both original choral pieces and arrangements for Hal Leonard. In addition, she works in association with the entire choral staff in the areas of product development, editing and marketing.

Widely recognized as one of the top educational choral writers today, Audrey composes music with rare beauty, simplicity and charm. She is a highly regarded educator, clinician, editor and producer.

Begin With the Beat

KEYS TO SIGHT-SINGING SUCCESS

- Create a positive classroom environment. *Be enthusiastic!*
- Either by means of a personal copy or by means of overhead projection, each student needs to have clear visual access to the reproducible exercises on pages 4 and 5.
- Students will gain the most from this series with consistent practice. Plan to spend at least 3 to 5 minutes on these activities each time the group meets. Regular, consistent practice is optimal.
- Be alert to student successes and sincerely praise students when they do well.
- Don't try to accomplish too much at one time. Learning to sight-read is not an easy task. The goal is *steady, forward progress*.

TEACHING CONCEPTS

With your students, read, briefly explain and demonstrate the concepts as they are introduced.

- **Steady Beat**
- **Quarter note ♩**

    Speaking Rhythms System: say "ta"

    Clapping Rhythms System: one clap

- **Quarter rest ⅜**

    Speaking Rhythms System: say "sh"

    Clapping Rhythms System: one shake (a gesture with both hands which resembles shaking water from one's hands)

    Choose either a speaking or clapping counting system for your students and stick with it.

- **Barline and Measure**
- **Repeat Sign**

TEACHING SEQUENCE FOR EXERCISES

1. Teacher establishes a slow, steady beat.
2. Students play the beat so that it is kinesthetically felt. Using the speaking rhythms system, students play the beat by lightly patting a hand on their lap. Using the clapping rhythms system, students play the beat by lightly tapping their foot.
3. Teacher provides preparatory count-off, "ONE two ready begin" and then students speak or clap the rhythm of the exercise while at the same time playing the steady beat.
4. Once perfected *a cappella*, then students perform the exercise with the play-along CD accompaniment. CD 1 is a four-measure accompaniment and CD 2 is an eight-measure accompaniment. Use the appropriate track as indicated at the beginning of the exercise.

Begin With the Beat

EXERCISES

Keep It Steady

Just as our hearts beat with an even pulse,
the *beat* is the steady pulse which underlies all music.

Quarter Note and Quarter Rest

♩ = Quarter Note = One beat of sound

𝄽 = Quarter Rest = One beat of silence

Ex. 1

Barline and Measure

Barlines (|) are used to group music notes and rests together. The area between two barlines is called a *measure*.

Barline   Measure   Barline

Any number of beats may be grouped in a measure.
There are four beats per measure in the exercises below.

Ex. 2

Ex. 3

Repeat

The repeat sign (:|) is used to indicate that a section of music should be repeated.

Ex. 4

Begin With the Beat

EXERCISES

More Practice with
Quarter Notes and Quarter Rests

Play the beat as you clap or chant the rhythms of each exercise. Keep the beat steady!

Four-measure exercises:

Ex. 1

Ex. 2

Ex. 3

Eight-measure exercises:

Ex. 4

Ex. 5

Ex. 6

Challenge!

Ex. 7

Key of D
Add Do and Re

TEACHER TIPS

MORE KEYS TO SIGHT-SINGING SUCCESS

- Require each student to play the beat.
- Make sure each student has clear visual access to the reproducible exercises on pages 7 and 8 either with his or her own reproduced page, or by means of an overhead projector image. Repeatedly encourage students to focus on the exercise at hand.
- Maintain consistent practice. Plan to spend at least three to five minutes on these activities each time the group meets.
- Introduce concepts well, but be quick and succinct. Keep students involved in making music as opposed to discussing music.
- When a mistake is made, encourage students to keep moving their eyes forward in tempo and attempt to resume sight-singing through the end of the exercise.
- Continue to sincerely praise students when they do well.
- Refrain from singing with the students. Get them started and then let them proceed alone.

TEACHING CONCEPTS

With your students, read, briefly explain and demonstrate aurally the concepts as they are introduced.

- **Pitch**
- **Staff:** Explain that although the music staff is like a ladder, notes appear up and down on *both lines* and *spaces*.
- **Introduce *Do* and *Re*:** Make sure students recognize the difference between *Do* and *Re* both visually and aurally.

Note: If students have previous sight-singing experience with *Do* as a different note (such as Middle C or F), explain that *Do* may be designated as any note on the staff. *Re* will always be the upper next-door neighbor to *Do* regardless of which line or space *Do* appears on.

TEACHING SEQUENCE FOR EXERCISES

First begin with the rhythm alone:

1. Teacher establishes a slow, steady beat.
2. Students play the beat so that it is kinesthetically felt. Remember, using the *speaking rhythms system*, students play the beat by lightly patting a hand on their lap. Using the *clapping rhythms system*, students play the beat by lightly tapping their foot.
3. Teacher provides preparatory count-off, "ONE two ready begin" and then students speak or clap the rhythm of the exercise while at the same time playing the steady beat.

   Then do the exercise again adding pitch:

   1. Teacher establishes *Do* (D) aurally.

   2. Teacher provides preparatory count-off, "ONE two ready begin" and then students sight-sing the pitches (ex. *do do re re*) in rhythm while at the same time playing the steady beat.

   Once perfected *a cappella*, then students perform the exercise with the play-along CD accompaniment. Use Tracks 3 or 4 as indicated at the beginning of the exercise.

Adding Pitch to the Beat

Pitch is how high or low each note sounds. A music note is placed on the staff (≡) to indicate its pitch. The staff is like a ladder. Notes placed near the bottom of the staff sound lower than notes placed higher on the staff.

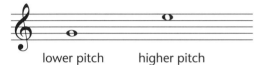

lower pitch   higher pitch

Introducing *Do*

Do is often the pitch which represents the home base, sometimes called the home tone or keynote. *Do* can be assigned to any pitch, but for now we will assign it to the pitch D.

D
Do

3
Ex. 1   *Sing:* Do

Meet *Re*

Re is the upper next-door neighbor note to *Do*. If *Do* is the note D, then *Re* is the note E.

D   E
Do   Re

4
Ex. 2   *Sing:* Do   Re

4
Ex. 3   *Sing:* Do

OK TO REPRODUCE

Add Do and Re

EXERCISES

More Practice with *Do* and *Re*

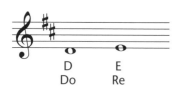

Ex. 1 — Do

Ex. 2 — Do

Ex. 3 — Do

Ex. 4 — Do Re

Ex. 5 — Do

Ex. 6 — Do

Challenge!

Ex. 7 — Do

Introduce Meter and Mi

TEACHER TIPS

MORE KEYS TO SIGHT-SINGING SUCCESS

➤ Be alert to student successes and praise them sincerely when they do well. Most younger children enjoy being praised individually. Older students often do not wish to be singled out among their peers, but they do, however, enjoy praise which is directed to the whole group.

➤ Create a classroom climate where mistakes are treated as challenges rather than problems.

➤ Refrain from singing with the students. Get them started and then let them proceed alone.

➤ Make use of the teachable moment. If students ask questions, provide more in-dept explanations.

➤ Allow a student to set the tempo and/or conduct the group through an exercise.

➤ Encourage students to **concentrate**, **Concentrate**, **CONCENTRATE** and make every attempt to sight-sing the exercise correctly the first time.

TEACHING CONCEPTS

With your students, read, briefly explain and demonstrate the concepts as they are introduced.

➤ $\frac{4}{4}$ **Meter**: At this time it is not necessary to go into great detail while explaining this concept. Students do need to understand the concept that in $\frac{4}{4}$ time, there will be four beats per measure.

➤ **Introducing *Mi***: Make sure that students recognize the difference between *Do*, *Re* and *Mi* both visually and aurally.

➤ **Half note:** ♩   **Half rest:** ▬
Speaking system: say "ta-ah"   say "sh-sh"
Clapping system: clap-squeeze   two "shakes"

TEACHING SEQUENCE FOR EXERCISES

First begin with the rhythm alone:

1. Teacher establishes a slow, steady beat.

2. Students play the beat so that it is kinesthetically felt.

3. Teacher provides preparatory count-off, "ONE two ready begin" and then students speak or clap the rhythm of the exercise while at the same time playing the steady beat.

Then do the exercise again adding pitch:

1. Teacher establishes *Do* (D) aurally. *

2. Teacher provides preparatory count-off, "ONE two ready begin" and then students sight-sing the pitches (ex. *do do re re mi mi*) in rhythm while at the same time playing the steady beat.

3. Once perfected *a cappella*, then students perform the exercise with the play-along CD accompaniment. Use Tracks 5 or 6 as indicated at the beginning of the exercise.

* Note that exercise 4 on page 10 and exercise 5 on page 11 both begin on the syllable *Mi*. Just prior to performing this exercise using pitches, point this out to the students. Explain that you will give them the pitch for *Do*, the home base, and then they will need to sing in their heads the pitch sequence: *do-re-mi* to find the starting pitch. In the beginning, demonstrate this aurally for the students. The eventual goal, however, is to have them find the starting pitch on their own.

Introduce Meter and Mi

EXERCISES

Time Signature: $\frac{4}{4}$ Meter

A *time signature* (sometimes called a *meter signature*) is a set of numbers which appear at the beginning of a piece of music.

4 The top number shows the number of beats per measure.

4 The bottom number shows the kind of note that represents the beat (4 means quarter note).

Ex. 1   *Sing:* Do   Re

Introducing *Mi*

Mi is the upper next-door neighbor note to *Re*. If *Do* is the note D and *Re* is the note E, then *Mi* is the note F♯.

D E F#
Do Re Mi

Ex. 2   *Sing:* Do   Mi

Half Note and Half Rest

Half Note   *Half Rest*

A *half note* represents two beats of sound when the quarter note represents the beat.
A *half rest* represents two beats of silence when the quarter note represents the beat.

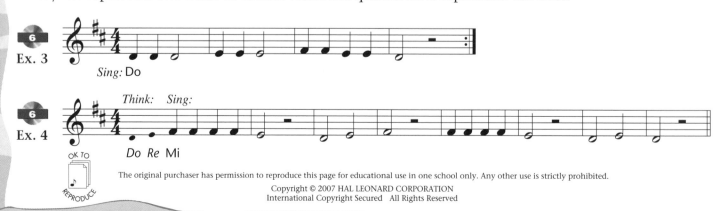

Ex. 3   *Sing:* Do

Think: *Sing:*

Ex. 4   *Do Re* Mi

Introduce Meter and Mi

Practice with *Do, Re* and *Mi*

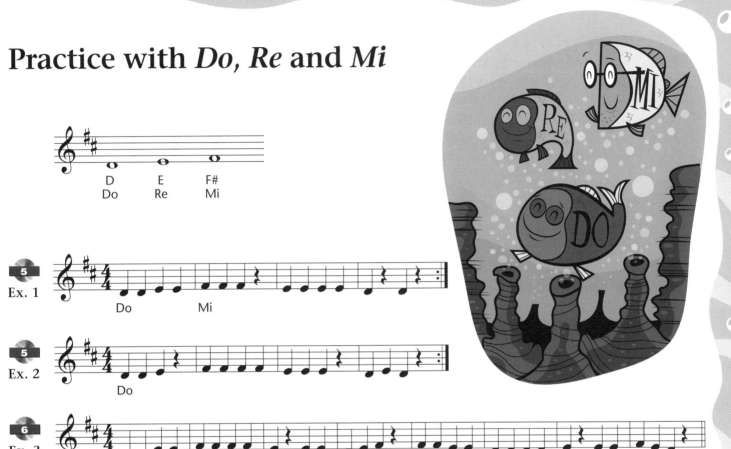

Practice with Half Notes and Half Rests

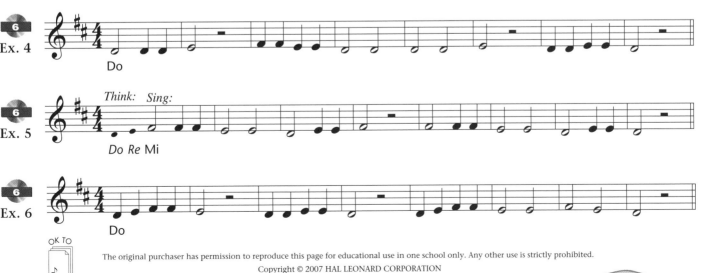

Key of D
Add Neighbors FA and SOL

TEACHER TIPS

MORE KEYS TO SIGHT-SINGING SUCCESS

- Continue to maintain consistent practice. Steady progress is the goal!
- Be sure to introduce concepts well, but be quick and succinct. Keep students *making* music, rather than talking about music.
- Develop a helpful classroom atmosphere where mistakes are treated as challenges rather than problems. Allow no student to make fun of another person's honest mistake.
- Challenge: Divide the class into two groups. Assign a different exercise to each group and have them sight-read these parts simultaneously. Choose exercises with the same CD number for harmonious part-singing.
- Challenge students by increasing the tempo of the exercise.

TEACHING CONCEPTS

With your students, read, briefly explain and demonstrate the concepts as they are introduced.

- **Adding *Fa* and *Sol*:** Make sure that students recognize the difference between *Do, Re, Mi, Fa* and *Sol* both visually and aurally.
- **Dotted Half Note:**
  Speaking system: say "tah-ah-ah"
  Clapping system: clap-squeeze-squeeze
- **Whole Note:**
  Speaking system: say "ta-ah-ah-ah"
  Clapping system: clap-squeeze-squeeze-squeeze
- **Whole Rest:**
  Speaking system: say "sh-sh-sh-sh"
  Clapping system: four shakes

TEACHING SEQUENCE FOR EXERCISES

First begin with the rhythm alone:

1. Teacher establishes a slow, steady beat.
2. Students play the beat so that it is kinesthetically felt.
3. Teacher provides preparatory count-off, "ONE two ready begin" and then students speak or clap the rhythm of the exercise while at the same time playing the steady beat.

> *Then do the exercise again adding pitch:*
> 1. Teacher establishes *Do* (D) aurally.*
> 2. Teacher provides preparatory count-off, "ONE two ready begin" and then students sight-sing the pitches (ex. *do re mi fa*) in rhythm while at the same time playing the steady beat.

Once perfected *a cappella*, then students perform the exercise with the play-along CD accompaniment. Use Tracks 7 or 8 as indicated at the beginning of the exercise.

*Note that exercise 3 on page 13 and exercise 5 on page 14 each begin on the syllable *Mi*. Explain that you will give them the pitch for *Do*, the home base and then they will need to sing silently in their heads the pitch sequence: *do-re-mi* to find the starting pitch. In the beginning, demonstrate this aurally for the students. However, the eventual goal is to have them find the starting pitch on their own.

Add Neighbors FA and SOL

Adding More Upper Neighbors

Fa is the upper next-door neighbor note to *Mi*, and *Sol* is the upper next-door neighbor to *Fa*. If *Do* is the note D, then *Fa* is the note G and *Sol* is the note A.

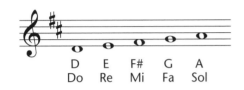

Ex. 1

Sing: Do   Fa

Ex. 2

Sing: Do   Sol

Ex. 3

Do Re Mi

Dotted Half Note   ## Whole Note and Whole Rest

Dotted Half Note   *Whole Note*   *Whole Rest*

A *dotted half note* represents three beats of sound when the quarter note represents the beat.
A *whole note* represents four beats of sound when the quarter note represents the beat.
A *whole rest* represents four beats of silence when the quarter note represents the beat.

Ex. 4

Sing: Do

Ex. 5

Sing: Do

Copyright © 2008 HAL LEONARD CORPORATION
International Copyright Secured   All Rights Reserved

D 2

Add Neighbors FA and SOL

EXERCISES

Adding *Fa* and *Sol*

Adding Dotted Half Notes, Whole Notes and Whole Rests

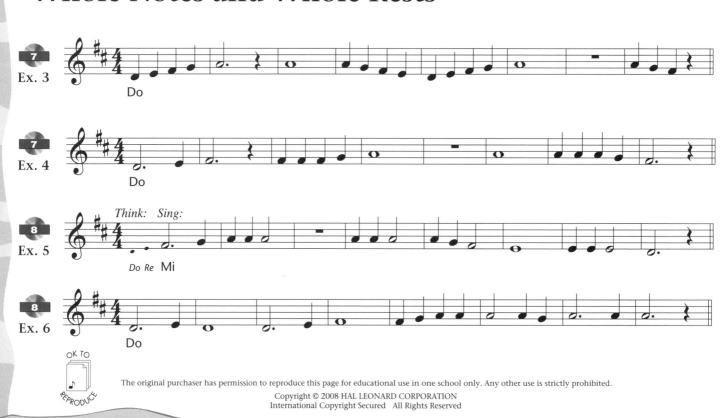

Neighbor LA Joins In

MORE KEYS TO SIGHT-SINGING SUCCESS

- Periodically review and practice previously learned exercises.
- Remember to refrain from singing with the students. Get them started and then let them proceed alone.
- Move among the students as they sight-sing to assess and help individuals.
- After a rhythm exercise is learned well, students often enjoy repeating the exercise again using an unptiched mouth sound such as "ch" or "ts".
- Accompany the students *ad lib.* on an instrument of your choice.

TEACHING CONCEPTS

With your students, read, briefly explain and demonstrate the concepts as they are introduced.

- **Eighth Notes:** Make sure students understand that eighth notes move twice as fast as quarter notes.
  Speaking system: say "ti-ti"
  Clapping system: clap-clap
- **Adding *La*:** Make sure that students recognize the syllable *La*, both visually and auarally.

TEACHING SEQUENCE FOR EXERCISES

First begin with the rhythm alone:

1. Teacher establishes a slow, steady beat.
2. Students play the beat so that it is kinesthetically felt.
3. Teacher provides preparatory count-off, "ONE two ready begin" and then students speak or clap the rhythm of the exercise while at the same time playing the steady beat.

Then do the exercise again adding pitch:

1. Teacher establishes *Do* (D) aurally.*
2. Teacher provides preparatory count-off, "ONE two ready begin" and then students sight-sing the pitches (ex. *do re mi fa*) in rhythm while at the same time playing the steady beat.

Once perfected *a cappella*, then students perform the exercise with the play-along CD accompaniment. Use Tracks 9 or 10 as indicated at the beginning of the exercise.

* Note that exercise 4 on page 16 begins on the syllable *Sol* and exercises 5 & 6 on page 17 begin on the syllable *Mi*. Explain that you will give them the pitch for *Do*, the home base and then they will need to sing in their heads the pitch sequence: *do-re-mi-fa-sol* or *do-re-mi* to find the starting pitch. In the beginning, demonstrate this aurally for the students. The eventual goal however, is to have the students find the starting pitch on their own.

Neighbor LA Joins In

EXERCISES

Quicker Rhythm – Eighth Notes

Two Eighth Notes (♫) = One beat of sound

An eighth note is a note that represents half a beat of sound when the quarter note represents the beat. Two eighth notes together equal one beat of sound when the quarter note represents the beat.

Ex. 1 (9)

Ex. 2 (9)

Adding Another Upper Neighbor: *La*

La is the upper next-door neighbor note to *Sol*.
If *Do* is the note D, then *La* is the note B.

D	E	F#	G	A	B
Do	Re	Mi	Fa	Sol	La

Ex. 3 (10)

Sing: Do   La

Ex. 4 (10)

Think: *Sing:*

Do Re Mi Fa Sol

Ex. 5 (10)

Sing: Do

Neighbor LA Joins In

More Practice with Eighth Notes

Play the beat as you clap or chant the rhythms of each exercise.
Keep the beat steady!

9 Ex. 1

9 Ex. 2

9 Ex. 3

Adding *La*

D	E	F#	G	A	B
Do	Re	Mi	Fa	Sol	La

10 Ex. 4

Do   La

10 Ex. 5

Think: Sing:

Do Re Mi

10 Ex. 6

Think: Sing:

DoRe Mi

Finish Off With Ti and Do

TEACHER TIPS

MORE KEYS TO SIGHT-SINGING SUCCESS

- Encourage students to imagine mentally how an exercise will sound prior to sight-singing it.
- Divide the class into two groups. Assign a different exercise to each group and have them sight-sing these parts simultaneously. Choose exercises with the same CD numbers for harmonious part-singing.

TEACHING CONCEPTS

With your students, read, briefly explain and demonstrate the concepts as they are introduced.

- **Adding *Ti* and High *Do*:** Make sure that students recognize *Ti* and high *Do* both visually and aurally. Let them hear *Do* and high *Do* simultaneously, so they can hear the octave. Explain that when sight-singing, high *Do* is simply sung, *"Do"*.
Optional: Explain and demonstrate the concept that the pattern continues on above high *Do* and extends downward below *Do*.

- **Skips:** It is important to solidly establish these skips aurally in the students' minds prior to sight-singing the exercises. In preparation for the exercises, using the syllables, demonstrate skips between these pitches aurally in a variety of configurations. Then do various echo patterns with the students using these pitches.

TEACHING SEQUENCE FOR EXERCISES

First begin with the rhythm alone:

1. Teacher establishes a slow, steady beat.
2. Students play the beat so that it is kinesthetically felt.
3. Teacher provides preparatory count-off, "ONE two ready begin" and then students speak or clap the rhythm of the exercise while at the same time playing the steady beat.

Then do the exercise again adding pitch:

1. Teacher establishes *Do* (D) aurally.*
2. Teacher provides preparatory count-off, "ONE two ready begin" and then students sight-sing the pitches in rhythm while at the same time playing the steady beat.

Once perfected *a cappella*, then students perform the exercise with the play-along CD accompaniment. Use Tracks 11 or 12 as indicated at the beginning of the exercise.

* Note that exercise 2 on page 19 begins on the syllable *Mi* and exercises 1 and 3 on page 20 each begin on the syllable *Sol*. Explain that you will give them the pitch for *Do*, the home base and then they will need to sing in their heads the pitch sequence: *do-re-mi* or *do-re-mi-fa-sol* to find the starting pitch.

WHEN I SING

On pages 21-22, there is a new song that incorporates the sight-singing skills that have been learned after completing these six lessons. Introduce the two staves, pointing out that they will be learning the music in the top staff only at first. Follow the same sight-singing sequence as has been used for the previous exercises. You may wish to divide the piece into segments (such as 16 measures) and have students completely learn one segment before moving on to the next. Once perfected *a cappella*, then increase the tempo. Then have the students perform the song with the CD accompaniment on track 14. (NOTE: a full performance version of the song can be found on track 13.)

Finish Off With Ti and Do

Adding More Upper Neighbors: *Ti* and High *Do*

Ti is the upper next-door neighbor note to *La*, and *High Do* is the upper next-door neighbor note to *Ti*. If *Do* is the note D, then *Ti* is the note C# and *High Do* is the note D.

D	E	F#	G	A	B	C#	D
Do	Re	Mi	Fa	Sol	La	Ti	Do

11 Ex. 1

Sing: Do   Ti

11 Ex. 2

Think: *Sing:*   *Do Re* Mi   Do

Skips

As you know, notes step up and down on the lines and spaces of the staff, which is like a ladder. In doing so, melodies are created. Sometimes music notes move in *skips* rather than *steps*.

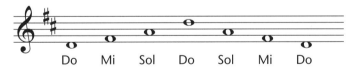

Do   Mi   Sol   Do   Sol   Mi   Do

12 Ex. 3

Sing: Do

12 Ex. 4

Sing: Do

D 6

Finish Off With Ti and Do

EXERCISES

Adding *Ti* and *Do*

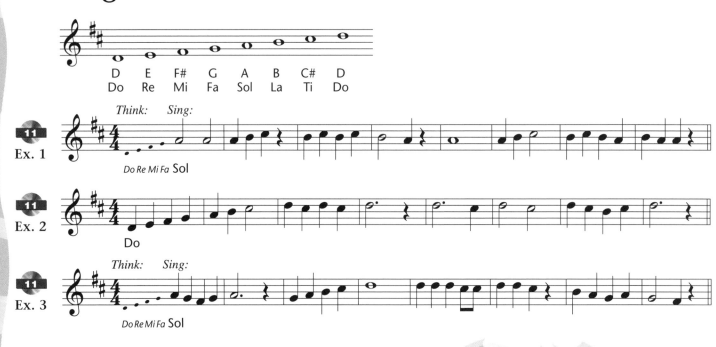

Skips

When I Sing

Words and Music by
AUDREY SNYDER

good for the soul, you know. La la la la,

good for the soul, you know. La la

la la la la, Raise your

la la la la la la la, Raise your

Part I **D.S. al Coda**

voice and sing with me! When I

voice and sing with me!

CODA

All

sing the mel-o-dy can chase a-way the blues, and my

heart is joy-ful when I_____ sing. And my

rit. 3

heart is joy-ful when I_____ sing!

When I Sing

Words and Music by
AUDREY SNYDER

Key of G
Begin With the Beat

TEACHER TIPS

KEYS TO SIGHT-SINGING SUCCESS

- Create a positive classroom environment. *Be enthusiastic!*
- Either by means of a personal copy or by means of overhead projection, each student needs to have clear visual access to the reproducible exercises on pages 27 and 28. Repeatedly encourage students to focus on the exercise at hand.
- Students will gain the most from this series with consistent practice. Plan to spend at least three to five minutes on these activities each time the group meets. Regular, consistent practice is optimal.
- Be alert to student successes and praise them sincerely when they do well. Most younger children enjoy being praised individually. Older students often do not wish to be singled out among their peers, but they do, however, enjoy praise which is directed to the whole group.
- Do not try to accomplish too much at one time. Learning to sight-read is not an easy task. The goal is steady, forward progress.

TEACHING CONCEPTS

With your students, read, briefly explain and demonstrate the concepts as they are introduced.

- **Steady Beat**
- **Quarter note** ♩

  Speaking Rhythms System: say "ta"

  Clapping Rhythms System: one clap

- **Quarter rest** 𝄽

  Speaking Rhythms System: say "sh"

  Clapping Rhythms System: one shake (a gesture with both hands which resembles shaking water from one's hands)

  Choose either a speaking or clapping counting system for your students and stick with it.

- **Barline and Measure**
- **Repeat Sign**

TEACHING SEQUENCE FOR EXERCISES

1. Teacher establishes a slow, steady beat.
2. Students play the beat so that it is kinesthetically felt. Using the speaking rhythms system, students play the beat by lightly patting a hand on their lap. Using the clapping rhythms system, students play the beat by lightly tapping their foot.
3. Teacher provides preparatory count-off, "ONE two ready begin" and then students speak or clap the rhythm of the exercise while at the same time playing the steady beat.

   Once perfected *a cappella*, then students perform the exercise with the play-along CD accompaniment. CD 15 is a four measure accompaniment, and CD 16 is an eight-measure accompaniment. Use the appropriate track as indicated at the beginning of the exercise.

Begin With the Beat

EXERCISES

Keep It Steady

Just as our hearts beat with an even pulse,
the *beat* is the steady pulse which underlies all music.

Quarter Note and Quarter Rest

♩ = Quarter Note = One beat of sound   𝄽 = Quarter Rest = One beat of silence

15
Ex. 1

Barline and Measure

Barlines (|) are used to group music notes and rests together.
The area between two barlines is called a *measure*.

Any number of beats may be grouped in a measure.
There are four beats per measure in the exercises below.

15
Ex. 2

Repeat

The repeat sign (:‖) is used to indicate that a section of music should be repeated.

16
Ex. 3

16
Ex. 4

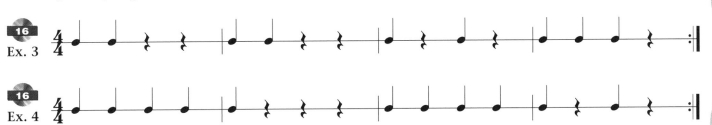

Begin With the Beat

EXERCISES

More Practice with Quarter Notes and Quarter Rests

Play the beat as you clap or chant the rhythms of each exercise. Keep the beat steady!

Four-measure exercises:

15
Ex. 1

15
Ex. 2

15
Ex. 3

Eight-measure exercises:

16
Ex. 4

16
Ex. 5
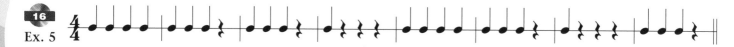

16
Ex. 6

Challenge!

16
Ex. 7

Add Do and Re

MORE KEYS TO SIGHT-SINGING SUCCESS

- Create a classroom climate where mistakes are treated as challenges rather than problems.
- Continue to maintain consistent practice. Steady progress is the goal!
- Introduce concepts well, but be quick and succinct. Keep students involved in *making* music as opposed to discussing music.
- Continue to sincerely praise students when they do well.
- Refrain from singing with the students. Get them started and then let them proceed alone.

TEACHING CONCEPTS

With your students, read, briefly explain and demonstrate aurally the concepts as they are introduced.

- **Pitch**
- **Staff:** Explain that although the music staff is like a ladder, notes appear up and down on *both lines* and *spaces*.
- **Introduce *Do* and *Re*:** Make sure students recognize the difference between *Do* and *Re* both visually and aurally.

Note: If students have previous sight-singing experience with *Do* as a different note (such as Middle C or F), explain that *Do* may be designated as any note on the staff. *Re* will always be the upper next-door neighbor to *Do* regardless of which line or space *Do* appears on.

TEACHING SEQUENCE FOR EXERCISES

First begin with the rhythm alone:

1. Teacher establishes a slow, steady beat.
2. Students play the beat so that it is kinesthetically felt. Remember, using the *speaking rhythms system*, students play the beat by lightly patting a hand on their lap. Using the *clapping rhythms system*, students play the beat by lightly tapping their foot.
3. Teacher provides preparatory count-off, "ONE two ready begin" and then students speak or clap the rhythm of the exercise while at the same time playing the steady beat.

Then do the exercise again adding pitch:

1. Teacher establishes *Do* (G) aurally.
2. Teacher provides preparatory count-off, "ONE two ready begin" and then students sight-sing the pitches (ex. *do do re re*) in rhythm while at the same time playing the steady beat.

Once perfected *a cappella*, then students perform the exercise with the play-along CD accompaniment. Use Tracks 17 or 18 as indicated at the beginning of the exercise.

Add Do and Re

EXERCISES

Adding Pitch to the Beat

Pitch is how high or low each note sounds. A music note is placed on the staff to indicate its pitch. The staff is like a ladder. Notes placed near the bottom of the staff sound lower than notes placed higher on the staff.

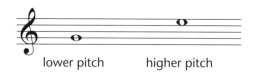

lower pitch   higher pitch

Introducing *Do*

Do is often the pitch which represents the home base, sometimes called the home tone or keynote. *Do* can be assigned to any pitch, but for now we will assign it to the pitch G.

G
Do

17
Ex. 1

Sing: Do

Meet *Re*

Re is the upper next-door neighbor note to *Do*. If *Do* is the note G, then *Re* is the note A.

G   A
Do   Re

18
Ex. 2

Sing: Do   Re

18
Ex. 3

Sing: Do

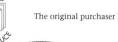

Add Do and Re

More Practice with *Do* and *Re*

17
Ex. 1

17
Ex. 2

18
Ex. 3

18
Ex. 4

18
Ex. 5

18
Ex. 6

Challenge!

18
Ex. 7

OK TO REPRODUCE

Introduce Meter and Mi

TEACHER TIPS

MORE KEYS TO SIGHT-SINGING SUCCESS

- Be enthusiastic! Continue to sincerely praise students when they do well. Create a classroom climate where mistakes are treated as challenges rather than problems.

- Encourage students to keep going when a mistake is made. Don't stop. Encourage them to keep their eyes moving forward with the tempo so they may resume sight-singing until the end of the exercise.

- Allow a student to set the tempo and/or conduct the group through an exercise.

- Promote confidence and success. Encourage students to **concentrate**, **Concentrate**, **CONCENTRATE** and make every attempt to sight-sing the exercise correctly the first time.

- Although entirely optional, the Accompaniment CD is a highly motivational tool for success.

TEACHING CONCEPTS

With your students, read, briefly explain and demonstrate the concepts as they are introduced.

- **$\frac{4}{4}$ Meter**: At this time it is not necessary to go into great detail while explaining this concept. Students do need to understand the concept that in $\frac{4}{4}$ time there will be four beats per measure.

- **Introducing *Mi***: Make sure that students recognize the difference between *Do*, *Re* and *Mi* both visually and aurally. Point out that the notehead determines the pitch; the note stem may go either up or down without affecting the pitch.

- **Half note:** ♩   **Half rest:** ▬
  Speaking system: say "ta-ah"   say "sh-sh"
  Clapping system: clap-squeeze   two "shakes"

TEACHING SEQUENCE FOR EXERCISES

First begin with the rhythm alone:

1. Teacher establishes a slow, steady beat.

2. Students play the beat so that it is kinesthetically felt.

3. Teacher provides preparatory count-off, "ONE two ready begin" and then students speak or clap the rhythm of the exercise while at the same time playing the steady beat.

Then do the exercise again adding pitch:

1. Teacher establishes *Do* (G) aurally. *

2. Teacher provides preparatory count-off, "ONE two ready begin" and then students sight-sing the pitches (ex. *do do re re mi mi*) in rhythm while at the same time playing the steady beat.

Once perfected *a cappella*, then students perform the exercise with the play-along CD accompaniment. Use Tracks 19 or 20 as indicated at the beginning of the exercise.

* Note that exercise 4 on page 33 begins on the syllable *Mi*. Just prior to performing this exercise using pitches, point this out to the students. Explain that you will give them the pitch for *Do*, the home base, and then they will need to sing in their heads the pitch sequence: *do-re-mi* to find the starting pitch. In the beginning, demonstrate this aurally for the students. The eventual goal, however, is to have them find the starting pitch on their own.

Introduce Meter and Mi

Time Signature: $\frac{4}{4}$ Meter

A *time signature* (sometimes called a *meter signature*) is a set of numbers which appear at the beginning of a piece of music.

$\frac{4}{}$ The top number shows the number of beats per measure.

$\frac{}{4}$ The bottom number shows the kind of note that represents the beat (4 means quarter note).

19 Ex. 1

Sing: Do   Re

Introducing *Mi*

Mi is the upper next-door neighbor note to *Re*. If *Do* is the note G and *Re* is the note A, then *Mi* is the note B.

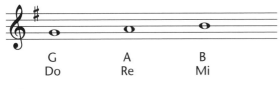

G   A   B
Do   Re   Mi

20 Ex. 2

Sing: Do   Mi

Half Note and Half Rest

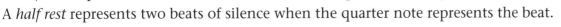

Half Note   *Half Rest*

A *half note* represents two beats of sound when the quarter note represents the beat.

A *half rest* represents two beats of silence when the quarter note represents the beat.

20 Ex. 3

Sing: Do

20 Ex. 4

Sing: Mi

OK TO REPRODUCE

Introduce Meter and Mi

EXERCISES

More Practice with *Do, Re* and *Mi*

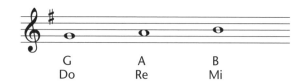

G — Do
A — Re
B — Mi

19 **Ex. 1**
Sing: Do

19 **Ex. 2**
Sing: Do

More Practice with Half Notes and Half Rests

20 **Ex. 3**
Sing: Do

20 **Ex. 4**
Sing: Do

20 **Ex. 5**
Sing: Do

20 **Ex. 6**
Sing: Do

Add Neighbors FA and SOL

TEACHER TIPS

MORE KEYS TO SIGHT-SINGING SUCCESS

- Be sure to introduce concepts well, but be quick and succinct. Keep students *making* music, rather than talking about music.
- When a mistake is made, encourage students to keep moving their eyes forward in tempo and attempt to resume sight-singing through the end of the exercise.
- Challenge students by increasing the tempo of the exercise.
- Promote student confidence by encouraging students to CONCENTRATE in an attempt to sight-read the exercise correctly the very first time through.
- Challenge: Divide the class into two groups. Assign a different exercise to each group and have them sight-read these parts simultaneously. Choose exercises with the same CD number for harmonious part-singing.

TEACHING CONCEPTS

With your students, read, briefly explain and demonstrate the concepts as they are introduced.

- **Adding *Fa* and *Sol*:** Make sure that students recognize the difference between *Do, Re, Mi, Fa* and *Sol* both visually and aurally.

- **Dotted Half Note:** 𝅗𝅥.
  Speaking system: say "tah-ah-ah"
  Clapping system: clap-squeeze-squeeze

TEACHING SEQUENCE FOR EXERCISES

First begin with the rhythm alone:

1. Teacher establishes a slow, steady beat.
2. Students play the beat so that it is kinesthetically felt.
3. Teacher provides preparatory count-off, "ONE two ready begin" and then students speak or clap the rhythm of the exercise while at the same time playing the steady beat.

Then do the exercise again adding pitch:

1. Teacher establishes *Do* (G) aurally.*
2. Teacher provides preparatory count-off, "ONE two ready begin" and then students sight-sing the pitches (ex. *do re mi fa*) in rhythm while at the same time playing the steady beat.

Once perfected *a cappella*, then students perform the exercise with the play-along CD accompaniment. Use Tracks 21 or 22 as indicated at the beginning of the exercise.

* Note that exercise 5 on page 36 and exercises 3 and 6 on page 37 begin on the syllable *Mi*. Also note that exercise 6 on page 36 and exercises 4 and 5 on page 37 begin on the syllable *Sol*. Explain that you will give them the pitch for *Do*, the home base and then they will need to sing silently in their heads the pitch sequences: *do-re-mi* or *do-re-mi-fa-sol* to find the starting pitch. In the beginning, demonstrate this aurally for the students. However, the eventual goal is to have them find the starting pitch on their own.

Add Neighbors FA and SOL

EXERCISES

Adding More Upper Neighbors

Fa is the upper next-door neighbor note to *Mi*, and *Sol* is the upper next-door neighbor to *Fa*. If *Do* is the note G, then *Fa* is the note C and *Sol* is the note D.

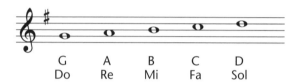

G   A   B   C   D
Do   Re   Mi   Fa   Sol

21 Ex. 1 *Sing:* Do   Fa

22 Ex. 2 *Sing:* Do

22 Ex. 3 *Sing:* Do   Sol

Dotted Half Note ♩.

A dotted half note represents three beats of sound when the quarter note represents the beat.

21 Ex. 4 *Sing:* Do

21 Ex. 5 *Sing:* Mi

22 Ex. 6 *Sing:* Sol

Add Neighbors FA and SOL

Adding *Fa* and *Sol*

G	A	B	C	D
Do	Re	Mi	Fa	Sol

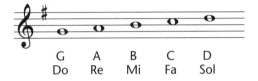

Ex. 1 *Sing:* Do

Ex. 2 *Sing:* Do

Ex. 3 *Sing:* Mi

Ex. 4 *Sing:* Sol

More Practice with Dotted Half Notes

Ex. 5 *Sing:* Sol

Ex. 6 *Sing:* Mi

Neighbors LA and Ti Join In

TEACHER TIPS

MORE KEYS TO SIGHT-SINGING SUCCESS

- Periodically review and practice previously learned exercises.
- Move among the students as they sight-sing to assess and help individuals.
- As students are ready, gradually skip steps in the sight-singing sequences.
- Discuss stylistic and/or instrumental elements with students when the CD Accompaniment Trax are used.
- Continue to sincerely praise students when they do well.
- Ear Training: When students are ready, challenge them to sing familiar melodies (for example, *Mary Had a Little Lamb*) using solfege syllables or numbers without printed music.

TEACHING CONCEPTS

With your students, read, briefly explain and demonstrate the concepts as they are introduced.

- **Pitches lower than *Do* – *Ti* and *La***: Make sure that the students recognize the syllables *Ti* and *La* both visually and aurally, and also in their relationship down from *Do*. For ease in learning, note that exercises 1 and 2 introduce *Ti* only and that exercises 3 and 4 then introduce *La*.
- **Adding high *La***: Now would be a good time to briefly introduce the solfége syllables of the major scale in its entirety. Explain that the syllables *do-re-mi-fa-sol-la-ti-do* are simply a repeating pattern from the very lowest notes to the very highest notes *ad infinitum*. Demonstrate this concept on a piano or other instrument. Slowly play at least a two-octave G major scale beginning with the G below middle C, saying or singing the syllables as you move up from note to note.

  Then introduce high *La*, making sure that students recognize the syllable both visually and aurally. Briefly demonstrate aurally the relationship of high *La* to low *La* (the octave) and both notes in their relationship to *Do*.

TEACHING SEQUENCE FOR EXERCISES

First begin with the rhythm alone:

1. Teacher establishes a slow, steady beat.
2. Students play the beat so that it is kinesthetically felt.
3. Teacher provides preparatory count-off, "ONE two ready begin" and then students speak or clap the rhythm of the exercise while at the same time playing the steady beat.

   Then do the exercise again adding pitch:

   1. Teacher establishes *Do* (G) aurally.*
   2. Teacher provides preparatory count-off, "ONE two ready begin" and then students sight-sing the pitches (ex. *do ti la*) in rhythm while at the same time playing the steady beat.

      Once perfected *a cappella*, then students perform the exercise with the play-along CD accompaniment. Use Tracks 23 or 24 as indicated at the beginning of the exercise.

* Note that exercise 6 on page 40 begins on the syllable *Mi*. Just prior to performing this exercise using pitches, point this out to the students. Explain that you will give them the pitch for *Do*, the home base, and then they will need to sing in their heads the pitch sequence: *do-re-mi* to find the starting pitch. In the beginning, demonstrate this aurally for the students. The eventual goal, however, is to have them find the starting pitch on their own.

Neighbors LA and Ti Join In

Down from *Do* – Adding Lower Neighbors: *Ti* and *La*

Ti is the lower next-door neighbor to *Do*. *La* is the lower next-door neighbor to *Ti*.

If *Do* is the note G, then *Ti* is the note F♯ and *La* is the note E.

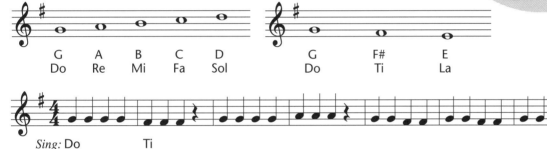

Ex. 1 *Sing:* Do ... Ti

Ex. 2 *Sing:* Do

Ex. 3 *Sing:* Do ... La

Ex. 4 *Sing:* Do

Adding Another Upper Neighbor: High *La*

High *La* is the upper next-door neighbor to *Sol*. If *Do* is the note G, then high *La* is the note E.

Ex. 5 *Sing:* Do ... La

Neighbors LA and TI Join In

EXERCISES

More Practice with *La* and *Ti*

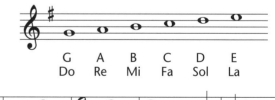

G — Do
F# — Ti
E — La

23 Ex. 1
Sing: Do   Ti

24 Ex. 2
Sing: Do

23 Ex. 3
Sing: Do   La

24 Ex. 4
Sing: Do

More Practice with High *La*

G — Do
A — Re
B — Mi
C — Fa
D — Sol
E — La

23 Ex. 5
Sing: Do   La

24 Ex. 6
Sing: Mi

Finish Off With Quicker Rhythms and Skips

TEACHER TIPS

MORE KEYS TO SIGHT-SINGING SUCCESS

- Encourage students to imagine mentally how an exercise will sound prior to sight-singing it.
- Accompany the students *ad lib.* on an instrument of your choice, or choose a student to accompany the group.
- After a rhythm exercise is learned well, students often enjoy repeating the exercise again using an unpitched mouth sound such as "ch" or "ts".

TEACHING CONCEPTS

With your students, read, briefly explain and demonstrate the concepts as they are introduced.

- **Eighth Notes:** Make sure that students understand that eighth notes move twice as fast as quarter notes.
  Speaking system: say "ti-ti"
  Clapping system: clap-clap
- **Skips:** Briefly explain and demonstrate aurally how melodies move stepwise up and down (such as what they have learned thus far) and by skips. Make sure that students recognize these skips from *do-mi-sol-mi-do* both visually and aurally.

TEACHING SEQUENCE FOR EXERCISES

First begin with the rhythm alone:

1. Teacher establishes a slow, steady beat.
2. Students play the beat so that it is kinesthetically felt.
3. Teacher provides preparatory count-off, "ONE two ready begin" and then students speak or clap the rhythm of the exercise while at the same time playing the steady beat.

Then do the exercise again adding pitch:

1. Teacher establishes *Do* (G) aurally.
2. Teacher provides preparatory count-off, "ONE two ready begin" and then students sight-sing the pitches in rhythm while at the same time playing the steady beat.

Exercises 3-5 (page 42): It is important to have the students first practice the rhythm only, and then go back and add pitch on these exercises.

Once perfected *a cappella*, then students perform the exercise with the play-along CD accompaniment. Use Tracks 25 or 26 as indicated at the beginning of the exercise.

MY SONG

On pages 44-45, there is a new song that incorporates the sight-singing skills that have been learned after completing these 6 lessons. Point out the use of top notes and stems up for Part 1 and bottom notes and stems down for Part 2. Notice the optional three-part harmony near the end. Follow the same sight-singing sequence as has been used for the previous exercises. You may wish to divide the piece into segments (such as 8 or 12 measures) and have students completely learn one segment before moving to the next. Once perfected *a cappella*, then increase the tempo. Then have the students perform the song with the CD accompaniment, Track 28. (NOTE: a full performance version of the song can be found on Track 27.)

EXERCISES

Quick Rhythms – Eighth Notes

♪ ♪ = *Two eighth notes* = One beat of sound

An *eighth note* is a note that represents half a beat of sound when the quarter note represents the beat. Two eighth notes together equal one beat of sound when the quarter note represents the beat.

25 Ex. 1

25 Ex. 2

26 Ex. 3   *Sing:* Do

Skips

As you know, notes step up and down on the lines and spaces of the staff, which is like a ladder. In doing so, melodies are created. Sometimes music notes move in *skips* rather than *steps*.

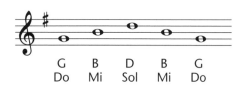

G	B	D	B	G
Do	Mi	Sol	Mi	Do

26 Ex. 4   *Sing:* Do   Mi   Mi   Sol

26 Ex. 5   *Sing:* Sol

Finish Off With Quicker Rhythms and Skips

More Practice with Eighth Notes

More Practice with Skips

Challenge!

27/28

My Song

2 measures introduction
With confidence

Words and Music by
AUDREY SNYDER

My song comes from deep in - side of me.

My song is my own mel - o - dy. When I am hap - py or

e - ven when I'm blue, I let my song come through.

My song, my song, yes, I have my

song. I **16** hum a lit - tle tune, what-
Loo

ev - er comes to mind; my heart makes up this
Ah

song of mine. **21** *mf*

Your song comes from

deep in-side of you. Your song is your

own spe-cial tune. When you are hap - py or

e - ven when you're blue, just let your song come

29

through. Your song, your song, yes,

you have your song.

a tempo

My song, your song, we all

have our song. Hm

My Song

Words and Music by AUDREY SNYDER